# LEARN THE VALUE OF

# Humor

by Ellen Kleckner

Illustrated by Dorey E. Evans

ROURKE ENTERPRISES, INC.
VERO BEACH, FL 32964

© 1989 Rourke Enterprises, Inc.

All rights reserved. No part of this book may be reproduced or utilized in any form or by any means, electronic or mechanical including photocopying, recording or by any information storage and retrieval system without permission in writing from the publisher.

**Library of Congress Cataloging-in-Publication Data**

Kleckner, Ellen, 1960–
  Learn the value of humor/ by Ellen Kleckner; illustrated by Dorey Evans.

  Summary: Presents situations that demonstrate the meaning and importance of humor.
  1. Wit and humor—Philosophy—Juvenile literature.  [1. Wit and humor.  2. Conduct of life.]  I. Evans, Dorey, ill.  II. Title.  III. Title: Humor.
PN6149.P5K54   1989      128'.3—dc19         89-24030
ISBN 0-86592-399-X

# Humor

Do you know what **humor** is?

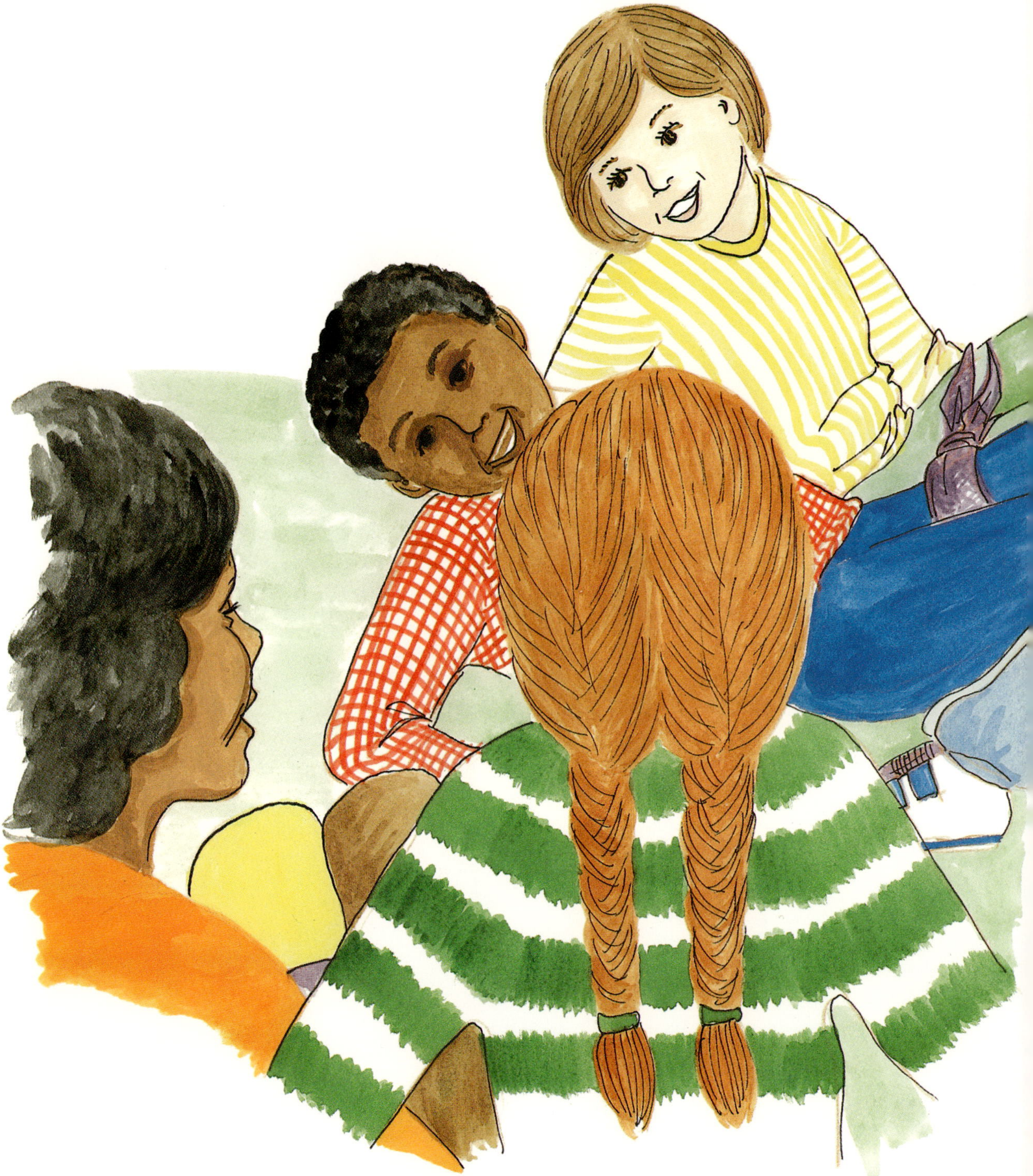

**Humor** is the feeling you get that makes you want to laugh when everyone falls down in a three-legged race and no one wins.

When you laugh at a dancing bear puppet, you're letting people know that you have a sense of **humor.**

Doing something silly like standing on your head is **humorous.**

**Humor** is putting on your clothes all mixed up to make your mom laugh when her day isn't going well.

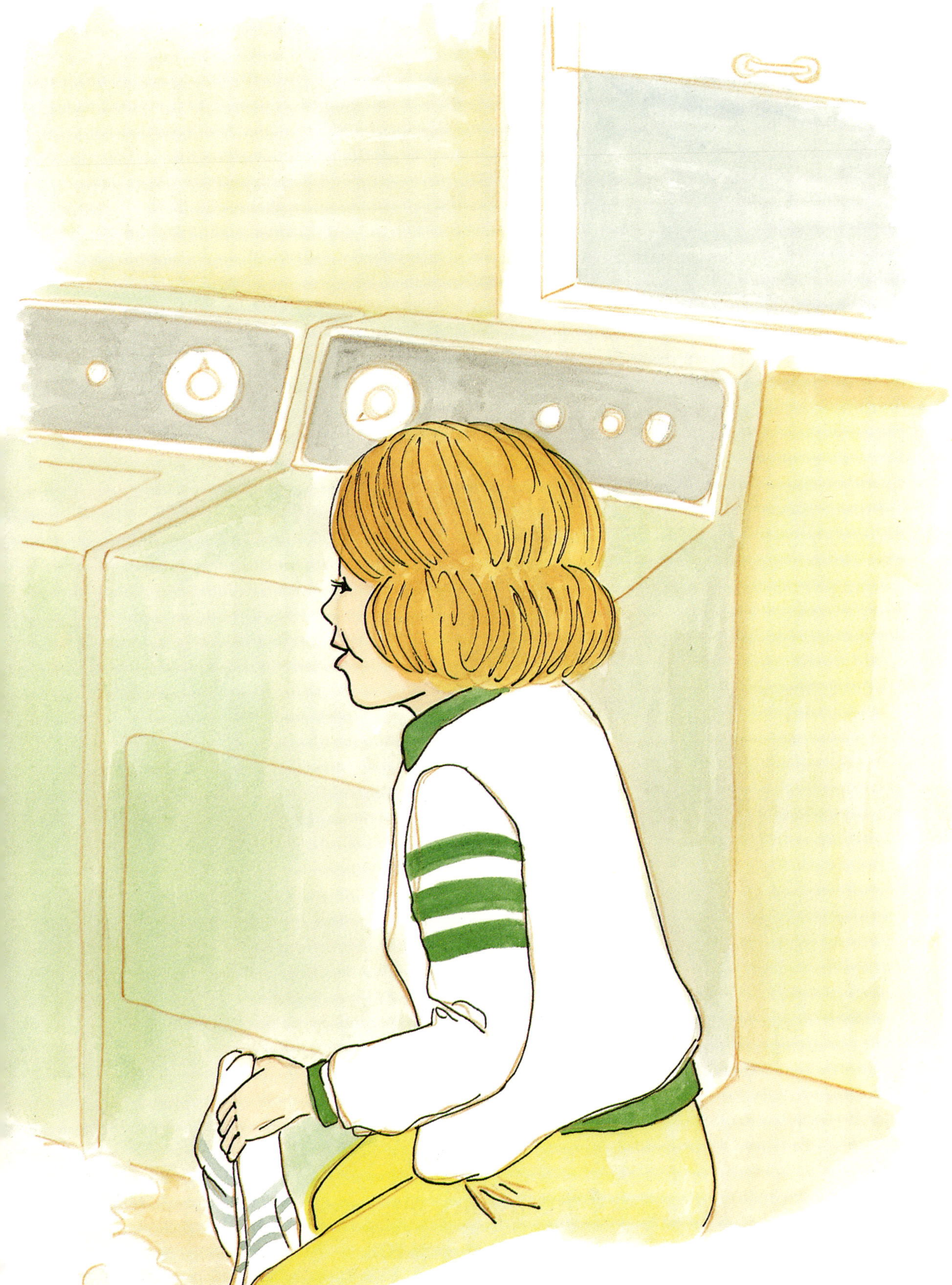

A magician's tricks are **humorous** enough to make children in the hospital feel better.

13

You're using your sense of **humor** when you write a story about watermelons on roller skates.

Laughing at yourself when you pour orange juice on your cereal by mistake shows you have a sense of **humor.**

Your teacher is showing her sense of **humor** when she laughs after you call her Mommy instead of Mrs. Katz.

Making funny faces in the mirror during a thunder storm brings out your sense of **humor,** and makes your little brother feel less afraid of the lightning and thunder.

Pretending the audience is wearing funny masks is **humorous,** and it can help you feel less nervous when you say your part in the school play.

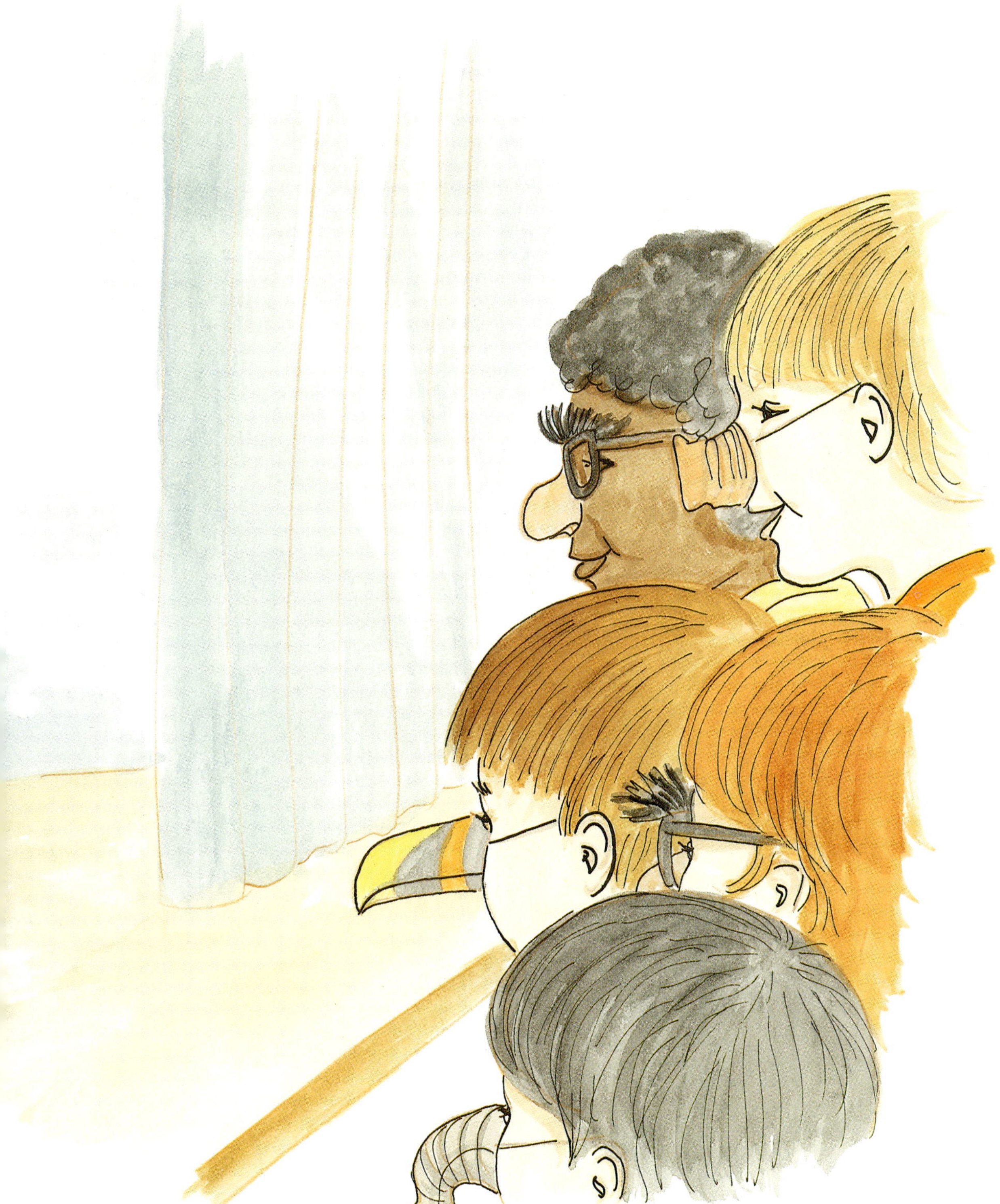

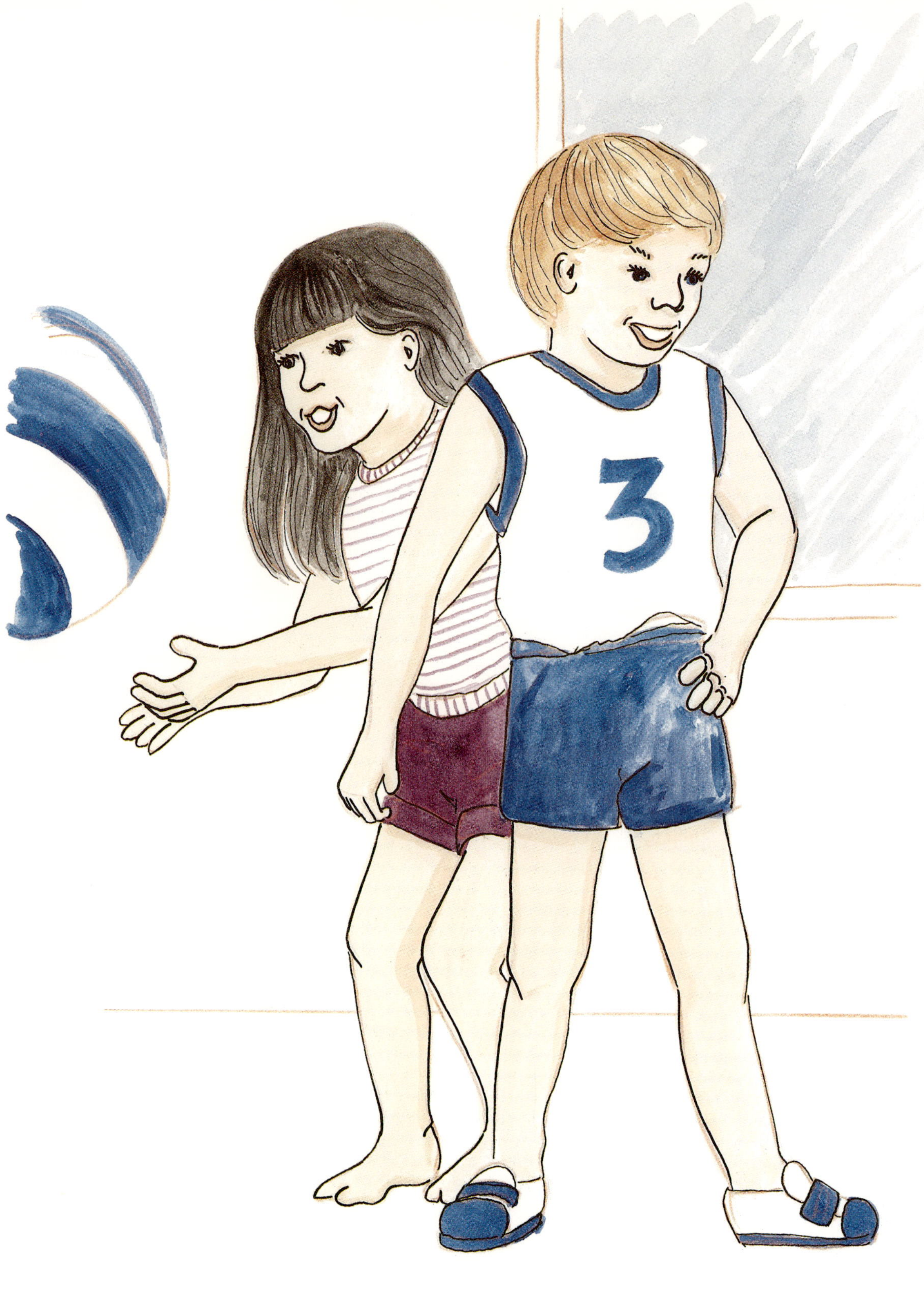
3

When your class trip to the beach is rained out and you bring the seashore indoors, that's showing your sense of **humor**.

You can share **humor** with a friend by telling him a joke you made up.

Decorating your dad's birthday cake in a funny way can bring out his sense of **humor**.

24

**Humor** is cheering up a sick friend by visiting her in the elephant costume you wore last Halloween.

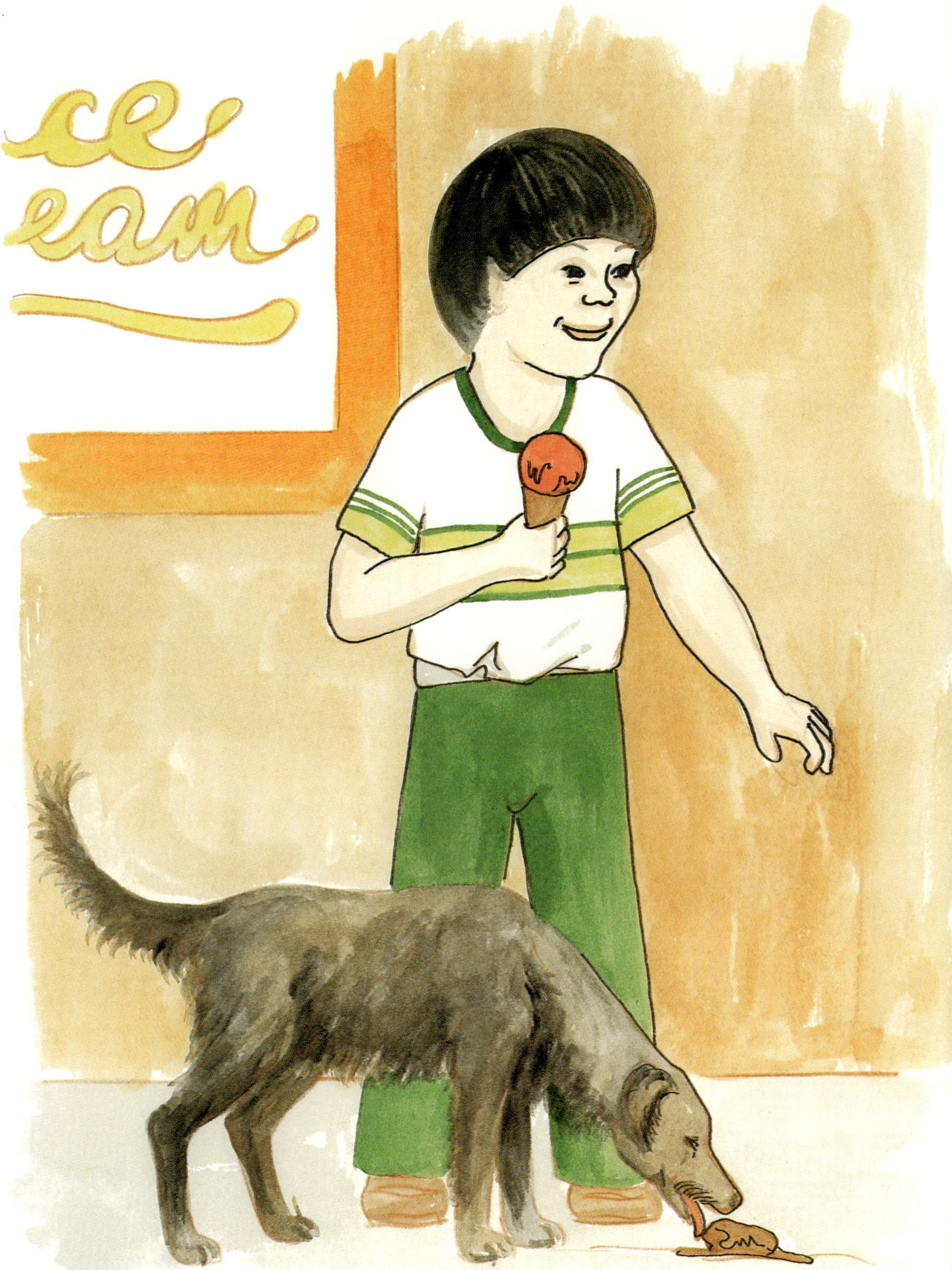
ce
eam

When your ice cream falls off the cone and Fido eats it, you're showing a sense of **humor** if you laugh and don't cry.

27

Circus clowns have a sense of **humor** because they do funny things to make children laugh.

**Humor** is drawing a funny card and sending it to your friend—just for fun.

**Humor** is being able to laugh and laugh—
just because it makes you feel good.

# Humor

It was Fun Day at Burr School. The children were allowed to dress up in any way they liked. The class that made Mr. Brown, the principal, laugh the most would win a prize.

The children gathered on the playground. They were ready to begin the Fun Day parade. Mr. Brown was ready too.

Kindergarten children marched first. They were dressed as pumpkins, lions, and elves. Mr. Brown clapped. Then came the first and second grades. Everyone had a funny costume. All the third grade children were dressed as California raisins! Mr. Brown couldn't stop laughing and clapping. At the end of the parade Mr. Brown went to the microphone.

"Boys and girls, this was my best day at Burr School. You all have a sense of **humor**," said Mr. Brown. "Everyone wins the prize. Laughter is the best medicine for making people feel good. And you all made me feel good today."

How does laughter make people feel better?

What are some things you've done that show you have a sense of **humor**?

# Humor

After breakfast Lisa grabbed her hat and baseball glove and ran to the park to meet her friends.

When Lisa arrived, Dave whispered to Ellen, "I wonder why Lisa is wearing a hat on such a hot day. Watch me when Lisa runs to first base."

Dave winked at Ellen when Lisa hit the ball. Just as Lisa reached first base, Dave pulled the hat off her head.

"What happened to your beautiful long hair," shouted the players. "What a haircut!" Lisa left the game in tears.

That afternoon Felix, the team's catcher, went to visit Lisa. He was wearing a big hat.

"Why are you wearing that hat?" asked Lisa. When Felix took off his hat, he had a pink bow in his hair. Lisa laughed and laughed.

"Keep the bow," said Felix. "It will look great with your new haircut."

How did Felix use **humor** to help Lisa feel better?

Was Dave using his sense of **humor** or was he just teasing Lisa? What is the difference?